FAITH

An Interactive Pursuit

FAITH

An Interactive Pursuit

John Blair

atmosphere press

Published by Atmosphere Press

Cover design by Senhor Tocas

Atmospherepress.com

CHAPTER 1
Pointing Your Effort in a Spiritual Direction

In the beginning God Created the Heavens and the Earth. (Gen. 1:1)

Man has spent centuries searching for meaning, wealth, relevance, direction, acceptance and love. His pursuit has taken him from one operational life modality (a way to live one's lives) to another. Each perspective, philosophy, pagan dogma, or ritualism teaches that it is the way to find the goals of peace, enlightenment, prosperity, spiritual oneness with the creator, etc. The keys to functional and spiritual happiness are often emotionally and financially costly. Through emotional and financial investment, the individual discovers that any of these modalities which promise so much tend to fall short when addressing the multi-variant complexities that compose the human condition. These complexities result from the very imperfections that make us human. Selfishness, rage, jealousy, stubbornness, lust, greed, gluttony, and avarice tend to muddle the individual's attempts to find happiness, peace and contentment. The Christian lifestyle classifies these complexities and self-centered responses to the travails of life as sin. This sin is, according to Christian teaching and lifestyle, the primary detractor from accomplishing a oneness with the creator and a form of holiness (we will dig into this in a great deal more detail later).

Many in the modern world choose to focus on and worship different idols within their lives. These idols can be jobs, monetary pursuit, alcohol, illicit or prescription drugs, sex, lovers, spouses, sports teams, individual sports themselves, hobbies, or emotional fixations that provide a target for the emotional and intellectual energies that the individual builds up over time. This idolatry is profoundly common in the modern world. Much of the general population and many in the church find these familiar pastimes and preoccupations to be a great salve of distraction from regret, sadness, hopelessness, disconnection, and despair that come from the disappointments of life. For example, the individual who has a hard day and goes to the bar to have a couple of drinks in order to "feel better." That individual relates alcohol or drinking with relaxation and de-escalation from stress and anxiety. This is merely one form of the rash of self-medications that individuals in America. The individual who has received Jesus as lord and savior still faces the temptation to indulge these simple idols and distractions. While Christianity has a well-developed doctrine and consistent teaching, the thorough and complete commitment that Christianity calls its members to undertake renders it as a complete lifestyle decision and commitment as opposed to a religion.

Christianity as Lifestyle, Not Religion

Many people have sought out the different religions on the planet. Some have chosen or been born into the Christian way of life. If one considers the broad directions and encouragements of the Bible, one must conclude that Christianity is a way of life, not a religion.

A religion gives rules for living. A way of life is a very broad philosophy adopted for the prioritization of things in and expectations of the individual in the areas of behavior, verbal interactions, spiritual focus, vocational priority, peer selection, time management and personal (faith) development. Keys to the Christian lifestyle include belief in the divinity of the Hebrew God and his only begotten son, Jesus Christ. Belief is not enough however. Acceptance of Jesus as one's personal lord and savior is also key. Submission of one's life and will to the perfect will of God through Christ is also necessary for salvation as any American Christian will tell you.

As a response to many of the feelings previously delineated, some believers have experienced issues with following through with the faith that they were taught as children. The modern world provides a cornucopia of alternatives for spiritual development or sense of purpose. Many seek spiritual peace, purpose or direction for their lives through faith in the substitutional sacrifice of Jesus Christ. For the purpose of this discussion, we will focus on the Christian faith in the United States. A serious analysis of the faith climate within the American church is necessary to assist the believer in achieving a greater understanding of Christian faith and how to develop faith further. In this book I will address several elements that negatively impact the faith of the individual believer:

*Reduced focus on God
*Distraction from the Path of Righteousness
*Corruption of Thought and Perception
*Negative experiences which can hinder Trust and thus Faith

In addressing these and other points which will come up in the discussion, let us first discuss some basic concepts that will apply to many who have done me the great courtesy of reading this book. As previously delineated, many divisions and sects of different religions have a presence within the American population. Additionally, a group of atheistic and agnostic persons also inhabit this country. Thus, the discussion that is laid out within these pages is virtually certain to either profoundly offend or bore to tears those who are not of the Christian faith. Given that that is the state of our discussion, let us begin.

Where are we going with this?

Many in this country have chosen or have been brought up to believe in a Supreme Being or God. The belief in the Judeo-Christian God is said to be essential to the broadly accepted faith of Christianity in this country. If one takes the perspective that the myriad of otherwise unexplainable events and convenient coincidences that Christians attribute to the divine creator, or God, are not

God breathed, then the explanations for such events are left into fields of chance and random occurrence. If this is the case, then chance and coincidence must be seen as often very fickle and pernicious factors. God's existence however is not a matter of empirical measurability but spiritual recognition. Spiritual edification and peace, which are profoundly subjective and immeasurable concepts, are the fruits of this spiritual recognition. Therefore, I must conclude, for the purposes of this discussion, that God does, in fact, exist just as the Christian churches on the planet assert.

The laws of the U.S. offer citizens a promise of freedom of religion. This freedom of religion has allowed the Christian church to grow unencumbered from government sanction. The growth of the Christian church in America and around the world will also be addressed in the coming chapters. We will be addressing this topic to ensure that a clear picture of the church and some of its attributes are included in our discussion of faith and the modern American church. Hopefully, this will give the reader a broader context when focusing on faith in the American church as well as their own personal faith journey.

The subject of Faith is one that encompasses the very core of our being. It has an impact on all our interactions as human beings. A key note to consider when initially addressing this subject is: Where do you, as an individual, stand on the subject of faith? In the modern world a great deal of time can be spent laboriously examining the arguments for and against the existence of a Supreme Being, or God. Some have argued that evolution and the "Big Bang Theory" sufficiently explain the creation and ongoing development of the universe. In so doing many of the "Big Bang" proponents have argued that since the "Big Bang" created the universe, God does not exist. Thus, evolutionists and deists have managed to separate themselves into two distinct camps. Many who can accept the existence of a supreme being are then posed with a much trickier question:

What in the world do you do with Jesus?

Jesus creates the most offensive argument for those who struggle with faith. He is the literal dividing line between Christianity and all other faiths. Who Jesus was/is resonates as the most profound spiritual question for both believers and seekers. Jesus was either a delusional megalomaniac or he is the son of God. It is genuinely that simple. For the church-going believer, Jesus is often seen as the Son of God. His actual intended role in our lives requires the believer to seek his righteousness DAILY. This very command requires the lukewarm or apathetic Christian to step up and give some of themselves into their relationship with Christ. Thus, passive Christianity is viewed by the church as a cheap knockoff of the faith the believer is called to develop through constant and deeply intimate connection with God through Christ. I have been rebuked more than once for decisions or attitudes which reflected a passive, docile or even negligent response to Christ's sacrifice on the cross. Negligent responses might include the response of a college friend. Let's call him Robert. Robert is a born-again Christian. He would consistently put himself into situations which would tempt him with sexual sin. Many of his brothers and sisters in Christ would encourage him to avoid those who led him into these situations (topless bars and strip joints, etc.). After a great deal of council, Robert separated himself from that group and repented for his lack of diligence. We are all subject to these periods or decisions which demonstrate either laziness or sloth in relationship development with Christ. We are called, however, to be diligent in avoiding them when possible.

So, if we conclude that the God of Christianity does in fact, exist, we must also come to terms with belief in scripture. The Protestant Christian Bible is composed of 66 different books composed over several centuries. It also imparts the only verifiable story of the genesis of an entire race and nation. The Bible also tells the story of a person whose appearance on the planet actually split our perception of time in half (BC/AD). Given that much of the Christian world considers the Bible the inerrant word of God, in this discussion I will take the same position. The importance of accepting the primacy of God through the mediation of the sacrifice of Christ at

Calvary is key to all discussions that follow. For the next chapters will include several discussions of issues of faith, barriers to its growth, the faith status of the American church, and a discussion of some trends within the church that have changed its demographics substantially over the past couple of decades. These discussions will hopefully allow the reader to evaluate his/her feelings regarding the health of their own faith and the status of their walk with Christ, and to gain an enhanced view of the present state of the church regarding faith.

I also hope to give the reader some insight into the demographic changes that have occurred over the past few decades within the broader church body. This discussion, I hope, will give the believer a broad idea of what the status of the Christian church is at the macro, or worldwide level. This will address demographics and philosophical trends within the church.

God's Requirement in Response to Christ's Sacrifice

The scriptures state that "For God so loved the world that he gave his only begotten son for whosoever shall believe in him shall have everlasting life." (John 3:16)

How do we as humans respond to this demonstration of vibrant, urgent and sacrificial love? For the Christian, a response to this often involves heartfelt worship and raucous praise. The Christian is also often called to deep devotion and faith via the Holy Spirit. The mother that prays steadfastly for the salvation of her son who has left the church is an example of this kind of devotional commitment. The daughter that prays for the soul of her alcoholic father demonstrates the kind of diligent love that the Christian is called to demonstrate on a regular basis. I can remember praying intensely for my children as they approached various life obstacles as they grew. The question of what to do about Jesus is often a quandary for many who struggle with faith. Many find that a belief in the Hebrew God is not that problematic until Christ is brought into the equation. Jesus stated "I am the way, the truth, and the light. No man shall see the father except through me." (John 14:6) Many who read this scripture might be challenged by this statement by Christ. It sets Christianity apart from all other faiths. It draws a very definitive line in the sand and demands a response of faith or non-faith, belief or unbelief. In the same way that the teacher calls out a student to grow and expand their understanding, so does Christ call us to build our faith with him as the chief example.

The exclusionary nature of Christian teaching brings into stark focus the importance of fervent and intentional adherence to scriptural teaching. In fact, Christ brought us two primary commandments that summed up the entire Mosaic Law. Love your neighbor as yourself and Love the lord your God with all your heart, soul, mind and strength. (Luke 10:27) These teachings mandate obedience. The obedience mandated allows the individual to remain in the will of God and experience tremendous faith-building opportunities in the process. Remaining in God's will allows the individual to avoid the consequences that inevitably come up when man is disobedient. Issues of punishment come into play as well as negative natural consequences. In obedience then the believer must reverently see God for who he is. God is the omnipotent creator of all that exists according to Genesis. He is also the benevolent God who sent Christ to sacrifice himself on the cross for the sins of all who believe in him. A key to remember here is that the benign, grace-laden God of the new testament and the Holy, detail-oriented and jealous God of the old testament are, in fact, the same God!!

One must eventually come to grips with a fundamental truth. The truth is this: The Sin of Adam in the Garden of Eden placed a spiritual chasm between God and man. This chasm is bridged by the sin cleansing and sin-nature-erasing sacrifice of Jesus Christ on the cross. The resurrection of Christ brought about the defeat of sin and death after his substitutionary sacrifice on the cross. Thus, at the final judgment, when the individual is judged, God will not see the sins of the person but the veil which presents the righteousness of Christ instead. Belief in the God of the Bible, the coming of the Messiah in the form of Jesus, his ministry, miracles, persecution, death, and resurrection are all vital components of faith for the modern Christian.

Scripture states "But without faith it is impossible to please Him, for he who comes to God must believe that He is, and the He is a rewarder of those who diligently seek him." (Hebrews 11:6) Without faith in these things, the believer is left with doubts and confusion. Doubts and confusion are not spiritually productive or within the will of God. For the lord is not a God of confusion and uncertainty but of clarity and purpose.

Is Christ Solely a New Testament Savior?

In many ways the consistency of God's perspective is also presented quite skillfully by Limbaugh in his exhaustive analysis of the Old Testament, "The Emmaus Code." Much of the Emmaus Code outlines and highlights the consistency of Christ's presence through-out each book of the Old Testament. Through all of the Old Testament, references to the existence, future, or spirit of Christ abound. The ability to see this has a lot to do with understanding the heart of the father is perfectly expressed through the attitudes, statements, love and tenderness of Christ.

In making this well-reasoned argument, Limbaugh accurately illuminates the reality that the kindness of tenderness expressed by Christ in the New Testament were also present in the Old Testament as well. The reality of an ever-present Christ as the only begotten son of God is a key lynchpin for the development of faith in the triune God.

You, the Triune God and Three Big Ideas

The relationship between God (the father, Son and Holy Spirit) and man rests on a singularly important set of four relational concepts. The absence of any of them renders the bond between God and man via the mediation of Christ depleted. The first concept is love. We are called to love God with all of our heart, mind and strength. This is a profoundly tall order in a world filled with distraction and disinterest in the spiritual. The culture calls us to love only those who love us. The culture tells us that those who love them that do not reciprocate are fools. Christ, however, calls us to love those who hate us. For Christ loved and died for the very men who beat him and put him on that cross. The men who were driving the nails into his hands had the opportunity to repent and see Christ as a savior in heaven. This is the love, brothers and sisters, that we are called to. Believe me brothers and sisters, I am in no way perfect in this manner either. I sometimes hate, loath, rage, and scheme wrongdoing for which I try to diligently repent and ask for forgiveness and additional guidance from the Holy Spirit.

The second is faith. Faith in the word and work of Christ is the foundation on which the relationship is built. The acknowledgement of the work of Christ and belief in the gospel that he taught are mandatory nuts and bolts for the believer. It is however a function of God's grace that the individual believer is able to believe in God at all. Scripture states that "faith comes by hearing and hearing by the word of God" (Rom. 10:17). For faith to grow the word must be heard. Acceptance, embracing, and clinging to the word are also essential in order for it to grow and take hold in a person's life.

The third concept is repentance. This concept calls for the believer to push sin out of the way and pursue the perfection of Christ daily, while renouncing the sin that attempts to hold one hostage in the power of Satan. The ability to see sin as a hindrance to the pursuit of Christ is a substantial form of grace. This sight is necessary if one is to understand the absolute spiritual dichotomy that exists between God and Satan. Repentance is often a very tough proposition due to certain sins which can repeat and repeat and repeat. In the face of these issues, additional time in prayer and scriptural investigation is often in order.

The fourth concept the relationship rests on is Obedience to the will of God through adherence to gospel of Christ. Obedience is that part of the relationship that in many churches is either overemphasized (to the point of legalistic ritualism) or disregarded completely (to the point of spoiled entitlement). The need to obey the teachings of Christ and the pertinent elements of Mosaic law become manifest when considering the words that Jesus often told those whom he healed. Many of Jesus's discussions with them ended with "...go and sin no more." This gives validation and surety to the Law of Moses which Jesus was sent to fulfill (Matt. 5:17).

Obedience is also the concept that sits on the backside of the grace relationship between God and Man. The grace found through the sacrifice of Christ on the cross comes with a call for diligent obedience to the Word and spirit of God. If sin occurs, repentance is then necessary. The faith that Christians are called to requires all different forms of grace throughout the relationship with Christ, from acceptance as Lord and savior to death and acceptance into Heaven with our savior.

A key to understanding the concept of obedience is the ability to perceive one's quintessential need for the loving mercy that God promises through Jesus. The mercy provided to the believer is made manifest through grace. This Grace is essential for our ability to interact with God in any way at all. Let's face it, we sin a lot! Sometimes intentionally, sometimes thought-lessly. Man's penchant for spiritual self-destruction is extremely well documented. Obedience requires man to take the priority off of his own desires and make the priority God's will and purpose. This ability to do that at all has also ZERO to do with God.

Being imperfect, we are instructed to call out to God and request spiritual intervention in order to combat the temptations and schemes of the enemy. Scripture calls you to recognize your sins when they occur. That is where faith in God's existence, purposes, and methods comes in. Then the love of the lord calls you to ask forgiveness through obedience to his direction.

Then the concept of repentance gives you that strong pivot foot that will allow you to turn from the behavior and avoid it moving forward. Repentance however is more than just a matter of will. It is a matter, in many cases, of filling your eyes or calendar with the work or things of God instead of the elements that triggered your need for repentance to start with.

Bonhoeffer argues that grace has been profoundly watered down over the centuries. We will launch into that weighty concept in the next chapter.

CHAPTER 2
A Question of Focus

The Relevance of Repentance

The ability to focus on the calling of Christ is addressed very eloquently by Dietrich Bonhoeffer in "The Cost of Discipleship." In it, Bonhoeffer asserts that there can be no obedience without faith and no faith without obedience. The interrelationship of the two concepts is at the root of Bonhoeffer's argument that true faith is a far more elusive concept than it is presented in the modern American church. He does not compare his German roots to America but does assert that his mid-20th century Germany struggles with the distinction between expensive grace and cheap grace. These terms differ in that cheap grace comprises forgiveness without the need for repentance and expensive grace is defined as grace which cost a man's life and requires repentance. This repentance is required because God is holy and demands holiness. God's requirement of holiness is not met by man as he is and thus a new covenant was needed between man and God.

Conversion of a Simple Kid

My own personal salvation story tracks back to February 1984 at a Wednesday night youth group that I attended at the behest of my then-girlfriend, Vanessa. She suggested I go to the "Youth Alive" youth group with her. It was an opportunity to spend more time with her.

So, I jumped at the opportunity wholeheartedly. Boy was I in for an experience. Up to that point my experience with church and faith had been scattered at best due to my parents' staunch disagreement over religion. Periodic trips to church over holidays had given me mild exposure to the actual practice of Christianity beyond being good and trying not to hurt anyone. The churches I did attend were very much about ritual and ceremony. The people at this youth group smiled at me! Many of the youth leaders hugged me upon introductions and told me that Jesus loved me! This was all pretty alien to my extremely stoic sensibilities. I got to my seat and music started to play. This was not church music though. This was cool! Vanessa got up and started clapping her hands and singing. I got up to and noticed that everyone was standing and singing. After several songs that lifted by granite spirit to an elevation I did not know I could reach: Mike Carlton got up and preached a message on the role of the individual Christian in God's master plan. He spoke of something called the Holy Spirit as if it were common knowledge. That Wednesday night that mysterious Holy Spirit (manifested through the voice and message of Youth Pastor Mike Carlton) looked me dead in the eyes and said: "I love you more than can imagine. I want a relationship with YOU. Your move." My relatively uneducated spirit had no other response but to rise very cautiously from my chair and walk down to the front as a room full of 350-plus teenagers watched. I truly do believe that Christ did not save me from bad behavior, poor choices, or evil intent. Christ saved me from a behavior pattern that was much more insidious: Apathy. Revelation 3:15-16 notes Christ's insistence on close relationship which I was completely ignorant of until that night. My new covenant was sealed that cold February night all those years ago.

This new covenant changes the nature of the relationship between God and man. God arranged for a single perfect sacrifice to be made for all sins of all people who have faith in the sanctity and validity of the sacrifice. God sent as the sacrifice the only one who could possibly meet the level of perfection in life that God's holy nature demanded. God sent his only begotten son. The second member of the trinity, the son, was sent to live a sinless life, satisfying the need for holiness. This sinless, spiritually perfect life was then sacrificed as Jesus's blood was shed on the cross. The creation of the new covenant was not complete, however, until on the third day Jesus rose from the grave in fulfillment of prophesies that were spoken about him. In his resurrection the defeat of death was complete. Christ perfectly met the holiness requirement in sacrificing himself for the souls of many. God's requirements in the post-resurrection church are quite clear. Love God with all your heart, soul, mind and spirit and Love your neighbor as yourself. These are the two primary commandments for all.

The Modern Church vs. The Book of Acts

The modern church in America struggles with doubt, mistrust, distractions, confusion and a serious shortage of faith according to a study by ARG whose findings are noted by Christianity Today. This statement is comparative of course. Comparisons of Church health on the meter of faith and focus can be made across centuries certainly. One can, for example, compare the Enlightenment Period and the Middle Ages regarding the writings and church movements that each period produced. In the Book of Acts the church is portrayed as seriously persecuted but lively and fervent. Issues of backbiting, gossip, and outreach logistics were very likely present in the early church. Scripture, however, paints a picture of a community of faith working together and supporting one another with a primary focus: the spreading of the gospel of Christ and the message of salvation by grace through faith in the substitutionary sacrifice of Jesus Christ for the sins of all and his glorious resurrection.

The single-minded focus the early church demonstrated was likely the product of several things. First, Jesus's ascension into heaven was a relatively recent event. Second, the memory and specifics of his teaching were fresh in the memories of his beloved disciples. The Romans and the Sanhedrin aided in the growth of the church and its laser focus. Though their desire was to destroy the church, the persecution of the church just fed the fire of the zealous apostles and their desire to bring the gospel to all the world. Third, persecution likely created curiosity in some that led them to investigate the speaking and teaching of the apostles at various points opening the door for the Holy Spirit to speak to them and call them into fellowship. Finally, the simple psychology of being told you can't believe something, or you can't say something can create a profoundly oppositional response which fuels growth in the targeted behavior.

Over time a great deal of spiritual passivity has overcome portions of the church. Many nations have laws which protect Christians from persecution. In these countries Christianity has grown in great numbers over the centuries since Jesus's Ascension into Heaven. These increasing numbers come at a cost in some cases. The specificity of doctrine within the teachings of the church has, from time to time, waned from very sharp to extraordinarily broad. Some might ask why. Some possible answers to this question include: the splitting of churches over doctrinal and other issues, varying social trends, and movements within the modern society which the church has had to respond to over the centuries. For example, I have seen a church split over affiliation with a larger church body. Some members wanted to be independent while others ardently sought to hang on to the larger organization. It is wise to note that church leadership changes over time in every church. Different leaders are brought in at different points for different reasons. These well-meaning men and women may well attempt to follow the leading of Christ and pursue after that leading diligently. Due to their different temperaments, however, they subject that church body to variation in their administration of the mandates of the church and interaction with the body. Leaders in the church can vary in their commitment to their position and the level of urgency with which they carry out their church-related duties. Church leaders can vary widely in their specialties regarding faith development, discipleship, and evangelism. These specialties, while normal, can create weak points within the individual church body as it applies to the broad-based Call of Christ to go and make disciples in all the world. I can remember being present when a beloved music director was removed from a church I attended (because Heaven forbid the church have upbeat music prior to the message—Heresy!!). This sort of removal of staff based on congregational temperament (or temper tantrum in some cases) does bring into question a couple of different types of protestant churches in this country. For churches can differ in what they view as their primary role in the development of the Kingdom of God.

Evangelism vs. Discipleship

The spiritual gifts of Evangelism and Discipleship have equal importance in the Body of Christ. The call to discipleship denotes a commitment to both, even though one might be gifted more profoundly in one area more than another. A noteworthy truth is that the call to discipleship should be responded to with tremendous diligence and fervor both by the individual believer as well as the church as a whole. Many churches pay particular attention to either discipleship or evangelism in America. The Evangelistic churches tend to focus on bringing people in and ensuring that the newcomer is given every opportunity to hear of the saving sacrifice of Jesus at the cross and his call to believe and be saved from the just punishment of the sins he has committed in this life.

Peter Haas of VitalMagazine.com summarized Rick Warren's *Purpose Driven Church*. He discussed Warren's outline of five themes that are part of being a Biblical Church in the modern day. These five areas are: **Evangelism, Discipleship, Ministry Opportunities, Fellowship, and Worship**. Haas defines Discipleship as "the adaptation of the individual to a biblical lifestyle." Evangelism is defined as "Sharing your faith in a fruitful way."

Many churches appear to proceed from the assumption that passive specialization in either Evangelism, Discipleship, or even Worship is preferable to a church that tries to give equal funding and fervor to each of the five themes that Mr. Warren outlined. In doing church this way, a congregation can grow extraordinarily large in attracting individuals that may very well be looking to Christ for just certain things like great worship or excellent teaching and discipleship programs. Churches that lean on "specialty areas" to sustain membership can run into issues when broader applications of the call of Christ are implemented.

Those churches that seem to specialize in discipleship have the same issue with overly focused thinking that the Evangelically-focused churches do. The discipleship churches can tend to devolve into "Christians Only Clubs." The fire needed to actually evangelize, and soul win is not a priority in some places. Some of these churches suffer from the same myopic tendency but in a different direction. The priority of discipleship is clearly mandated within the directives of Christ to the early church. The importance of consistent and thorough teaching development of spiritual disciplines is clear. Evangelism in the form of modern day "soul winning" has just as important a role. It is very easy for a church leadership to emphasis one area in which they have a strength and fail to address the shortfall in another area. This is true particularly when a congregation does not see the relevance of or have the stomach for the other areas of the Christian call.

A problem can arise however when a sacrifice is asked of the individual believer by the church body. How many times have we observed a believer leave a church due to a change in music, change in church personnel, or something similar? Christians in America change their congregation affiliation for a myriad of reasons.

Does this make them any less Christian? Perhaps it does not. It does, however, raise a question in light of the choice and action.

Church Hopping in Modern America

Many within the Christian church have moved from one church to another or one Christian denomination to another over the course of their lives. The frequency with which this occurs has not been fully studied to my knowledge. A question arises when considering the movement of Christians from one church or interpretation to another. Are we called to commit to a congregation and treat the decision with as little commitment as Americans apparently do? Or are we called (by God) to remain faithful to the church family that we are in? Scripture speaks of people being faithful and loving to one another in the spirit Christ taught them in the early church (see the Books of Acts and Romans). The Pew Research Institute Forum on Religion and Public Life investigated American Christian tendencies to Church hop and change faiths. The study, originally done in 2009 and updated in 2011, indicates that two-thirds of former Catholics who are no longer affiliated with the church left because they no longer believed in the teachings. Forty percent of them reported that they no longer believed in God. The report also indicates that many who were raised protestant changed faiths within Protestantism due to changes in life circumstance. Many reported a denomination change due to marrying someone of another faith within the protestant umbrella. The 2007 study reported that 28% of Christians in America left the denomination they were raised in. The survey also indicated that 44% of Americans now profess a religious affiliation different from that in which they were raised (PewForum.org).

The study also finds that of the 56% of Americans who are in the same denomination in which they were raised, 16% report that they had left the church of their childhood at some point and returned to it later. Thus, combined with the 44% that report being in another denomination other than their childhood denomination, 60% of those studied had left the church of their childhood at some point in their lives.

A significant question arises when reflecting on these staggering numbers. Has the size of the American Christian Church, in all of its divisions and denominations, made loyalty to the individual local church more difficult? It could be argued that the different denominations allow for the individual believer to find access to their God which will allow them to worship in a setting that is comfortable and acceptable to the believer. While this, on the surface, appears to be an innocuous perspective, one might ask, is it the path that the Lord intends to grow the believer in? This leads to an even deeper question. Is there evidence anywhere in scripture to indicate that growing in faith and as a believer is supposed to be easy or all that comfortable?

Many churches in America are growing to become massive collections of believers which offer significant positives and just as many significant negatives for the individual believer. Some of the positives include the availability of service and fellowship resources for the individual believer. These resources are particularly noteworthy when we remember that the Christian journey was not meant to be trapped in isolation but in community with other believers. Opportunities to connect to other believers in environments that foster the building and support of faith are often critical. Followers of Christ need discipleship resources. The pursuit of Christ in the heart of the individual requires diligence, sound teaching and application of spiritual truth as presented in the Bible.

Some significant negatives include the possible intimidation of the individual believer based on the sheer size of the church physical structure or the number of people within the service. Other issues of significant concern include a lack of access to church leadership, impersonal interaction with leadership when interaction is needed, and the difficulties to actually get assistance when "life happens," like a death in the family, a loss of work, a dry season in one's faith, or a bad diagnosis from the doctor. These are examples of times when a Christian needs the church to be the "hands and feet of Christ." A large church may have the resources to address such issues but must also have the people available who are able to meet the hurting or grieving believer in the middle of their circumstance and offer them a God-directed way through the circumstance or a strong shoulder on which to hold while the life storm rages.

CHAPTER 3
Spiritual Focus

Are we not called to Faith??!! Philippians 4:8 states:

> "Finally brethren, whatever things are true, noble, just, pure, lovely, or of good report, if there is any virtue and if there is anything praiseworthy-meditate on these things."

IF it is true that Jesus intended for us to avoid what some call "stinking thinking" (that thinking which reflects and reinforces a poor attitude and negative outlook), then it is also true that the Holy Spirit is more than capable of assisting the believer in avoiding the problems that come about from thinking in ways that do not honor God or lead to sin and the entertainment of further temptation. The entertainment of lustful thoughts for example can lead to obsessions, acts of fornication, or adultery. The products of obsessions, fornication, and adultery are destroyed trust, fractured or shattered relationship, bitterness, anger, and resentment, just to name a few. These types of situations result from choices which are driven by <u>perceived</u> need, entitlement, frustration or other pernicious maladies within the sinful human psyche. These are, at the end of the day however, CHOICES. The direction of Philippians 4:8 is clear. The entertainment of thoughts which do not edify one's spiritual walk can be potentially destructive in either the short or long term. It is important to seek God and ask for discernment when these very familiar and initially harmless distractions arise in one's mind. These distractions can wear down the vigilance of the believer and their familiarity can allow the believer's resolve and faith to be usurped. This usurpation is a very troubling in its manifestation. The usurpation of faith or distraction from faith can come from any direction or any form. It can come from the pretty girl that you finally get a date with. It can come from the spouse who persistently does not want to go with you to church. Distraction can be incredibly dangerous to the spirit of the individual. Clear and distinct understanding of oneself and your own particular spiritual weaknesses is always important when pursuing the spiritual discipline of the Christian lifestyle.

While understanding your spiritual weaknesses are critical to the pursuit of Christ, submission of personal agenda and self-interest to the felty of Christ is particularly essential. This can be a very difficult proposition for the individual with either profound trust issues or a significant need for personal control. It requires not only faith in the existence of Christ but also trust in God's will through his son.

The surrendered heart is quintessentially important to allow God to mold the believer into the masterful work of faith that God intends you to be. This surrender, while essential, is also very difficult for many to accomplish due to varied levels of distrust, disappointment, and wounds which the individual may have endured in life to that point of conversion. Surrender of agenda to Christ is subject to distraction at many levels but is still very necessary to being in a relationship with God through Christ and enjoying the blessings that flow from that relationship. This often takes the form of temptation to hold on to control of that element of your life that you surrendered control of at a more spiritual point.

It is said that if a disciple is devout of heart, then the lord will not allow more temptation than the individual can bear. In other words, there is always another option or a way out. Having the focus on the heart of Christ to make the Christ Centered Choice, however, is another matter altogether. Humans sin, it happens. We are called to the perfection of Christ via the Holy Spirit. The reality however is that we are totally and utterly dependent on the grace of God through Christ at all times. This dependence is a blessing to the believer for it releases the individual from responsibility for earning their own salvation or risking blowing their salvation through stupidity, arrogance, sin, or selfish insensitivity toward the father. A surrendered will and a contrite heart are said to be very pleasing to God.

The ability to surrender one's will on a regular basis is often a critical part of the discipleship process. The world around us scoffs heartily at the concept of surrendered will, particularly the idea of surrender to an unseen God. "Faith comes by hearing and hearing by the word of God." (Rom. 10:17). A very committed and regular "bath" for the mind in scripture would seem to be of the utmost importance to the believer when trying to stay in the will of God. It is a concept that has been somewhat neglected in recent years according to one study (see Huffington Post article April 4, 2013, it references a study done by the American Bible Society). This study notes that while 75% of those surveyed stated that America was in moral decline, 88% of respondents said they owned a Bible. Eighty percent think the bible is sacred. Twenty-six percent of respondents said they read their bible on a regular basis (four or more times a week). A majority of respondents age 18-28 noted they read their Bibles less than three times a year if at all. (The study was done by the Barna Group via 1,005 telephone interviews and 1,078 online surveys with a margin for error for the combined data as plus or minus two percent).

A point to examine is: why do so many Christians not utilize the spiritual tool that was given to us by God to counteract the schemes of the evil one? Have we, in America, lost the ability to recognize the profound danger in spiritual apathy? This is a key point in the analysis of faith in the church. The acceptance of what might be called moral relativism is a troubling trend in the American church. Some preachers refuse to preach on topics that might bring their congregations guilt (see Joel Osteen's position on preaching about Hell). The denial of or apathy toward uncomfortable parts of Christian theology has some very perilous consequences according to scripture. Affective idolatry in the form of doctrinal abandonment of some portions of scripturally validated Christian doctrine leads to the risk of spiritual death, see the old testament for proof. Let us also remember that the cities of the promised land of the Israelites were inhabited by other tribes and nationalities. The Bible reports that these tribes had indulged in actions which offended the God of Israel. How did God respond to being offended? Did not the God of Israel order the people of Israel to kill all in some of those cities? Thus, the ignoring of parts of the doctrinal teaching given by Jesus to his church would seem to be a very bad idea. The problem here, however, rests on a couple of fronts. First the average Christian appears quite susceptible to distraction.

A Closer Look at Distraction

Distraction in Modern America is a very common issue. Many children are diagnosed with Attention Deficit Disorder (ADD). Many who are not diagnosed arguably could be! The presence of day-to-day responsibilities can be overwhelming to some. Making enough money to pay the bills for things that are considered essentials in our culture is a significant problem for many in this country, Christians included. Crises like disease, emotional turmoil within relationships, and other individual-centered maladies can distract the individual believer and create large amounts of angst and frustration. The social issues of criminal violence, hunger, political disenfranchisement, and political and economic corruption can serve to rob the believer of the spiritual peace that Jesus died to give us. The other most obvious distraction is the overt temptation to sin which is always present in any interaction between imperfect humans or when thinking about anything that is not Christ. Given that distraction comes with living in a fallen world, it should be noted that it (distraction) should be accepted and acknowledged as a troubling reality within our world.

Could it be that the focus of the believer should be just on Jesus and his teachings? Scripture states that we are to focus on whatever is pure, just, noble, of good report and to think on these things (Phil. 4:8). In order to do this, the consistent renewing of our minds becomes critical. The renewing of our minds comes from consistent reference back to scriptural study and meditation. Without diligent scriptural study and regular meditation of God's Word, how is the mind of a believer to be renewed for good works through the spirit? The answer is quite simple, is it not! Thus, if an individual asserts that they believe the Bible, then the study and meditation of it should be as automatic as turning out the light when one goes to sleep. The Christian lifestyle is not intended to be a passive exercise. Intentionality is key in addressing scripture study. Paul mentions "the sword of the spirit which is the word of God." (Ephesians 6:17). If one were to study that set of scriptures carefully a critical point becomes clear. In all the armor mentioned in that discussion, the only actual offensive weapon is the word of God. Every other element mentioned is protective. This would seem to indicate that we are to use scripture to stand on the promises that God made in those pages. We would then be called to claim them through the spirit. Claiming the peace, joy, love, and self-control of Christ in our own lives and standing on that claim through faith is what we are to do. The Lord seeks those that worship him in spirit and in truth (John 4:24). The believer must realize that this world is not our home, but it is, in fact, in Heaven.

If it is the case that Heaven is our actual home, then Christians are merely tourists on this planet. We, as humans, were given dominion over the Earth in the garden of Eden. Then Adam surrendered that dominion to Satan via the original sin. Christians are not meant to simply live moral lives which deny them sinful pleasure then simply die, either. The Christian has a weapon in his spiritual arsenal to contend with the temptations, distractions, and sinfulness of this world. It is the Holy Spirit! We are to fight against the power of evil utilizing the Holy Spirit and the Word of God. But we are not to treat this world as our final destination. For if we did, it would lead us to fully partake in all the pleasures and indulgences that this world has to offer. These pleasures and indulgences would then, no doubt, lead to sin and a falling away from the calling of Christ.

The temptation of distraction can be extremely subtle for a believer. In the business of life, the pursuits of love, sex, wealth, influence, respect, comfort, and success are all heartily embraced by this world. The world, due to the fall of man and acclimation to the sin nature, has established the pursuit of the previously mentioned goals as norms which run in direct contradiction to sound scriptural truth and spiritual growth. As a result of this fact, tribulation is considered a necessary circumstance for the modern Christian to contend with. This tribulation is the result of the conflict between the goals embraced by the world (e.g., sex, money, power, stability, relevance, control, influence, etc.) and the goals embraced by the teachings of Christ (e.g., love mercy, peace, kindness, charity, self-control). The emotion-laden decision making that often results from this tribulation determines, for many, the path that they follow, or the priority manifested in one's own heart. Decisions consistent with the teachings of Christ bring a growing closeness to Christ and increased sensitivity to the Holy Spirit.

Increased sensitivity to the Holy Spirit brings with it the reward of discernment and greater understanding of the actual will and intent of the father in various circumstances that come up in the life of the modern Christian. This discernment can come, for example, in the ability to see options for decisions from the perspective of one's understanding of the will of God as to each options propagation of love, peace, charity, mercy, kindness and self-control. The key is the prioritization of pursuing God's will in the actual decision and seeking out his wisdom in the process of making the decision. The gift of discernment often comes from diligent study of the word (spiritual fencing if you will) and diligent prayer.

American Culture, Diligent Prayer, and Cultural ADD

It could be argued that prayer has become a passive and somewhat trite piece of American Christianity. One could challenge whether or not the average American Christian has the attention span or patience to pray as the saints of the past prayed for various things. We, as a society, have developed a cultural-level case of ADD particularly as it applies to spiritual matters and interactions with God. Our impatience in petitioning the throne of God is a particularly troublesome issue. The truth that God's time is not our time cannot be understated when working with new Christians as well as with seasoned ones. Many Christians will make a request of God without the least concern as to what God's will or opinion is regarding the element asked for. Some will pray for something a couple of times, it does not immediately arrive or occur, then they either question God's existence, his love for them, or his timing. Jesus calls us to pray without ceasing. We have been taught via parable the virtue of persistent prayer to the father. Sometimes the answer is long in coming because God may agree with our request but that the timing of its delivery must be perfect. For example, a man prays for a job for months as he interviews with various companies. He is hired by a company that is a perfect fit for him. Waiting on the Lord can try patience but is rewarded as faithfulness and diligence is shown in one's pursuit of God's will for your life.

American culture has embraced a spiritual relativism which runs profoundly contrary to the teaching of the Bible. The teachings of scripture are not to be watered down or sculpted into some pre-fabrication to fit into a section of broader experience. For the Christian isn't the relationship with God through Christ supposed to be THE experience of life?? While this predictably flies in the face of modern culture with its ravenous pursuit of money, fame, power, or borderline narcissistic self-empowerment, it also flies in the face of the overly expedient interpretations of scripture such as the "prosperity gospel" and other "feel good" scriptural interpretations which assert that God wants everyone wealthy, successful, and perpetually happy. These teachings conveniently avoid the actual life circumstances of Jesus's followers, Jesus himself, or innumerable followers in the old testament.

CHAPTER 4
Trust

We are called to trust in the lord. How do we trust in something you cannot see? Is this not the very definition of faith? So then the question becomes how does one develop faith. Scripture helps us here. The answer there lies at Romans 10:17. The root for trust and faith's building blocks resides in the hearing and practice of the word of God. Trials and tribulation tend to build trust in the lord and faith in his actions and purposes. Taking that initial leap can be a very traumatic proposition given the trials previously experienced in one's life. Though trials and testing occur, Trust in the lord and faith in his love and purposes still comes down to a decision in the heart of the individual: Do you trust in the purposes and long-term agenda of God? If so, then how willing are you to actively engage in the plan and work of building God's kingdom?

In participating in the building of God's kingdom, you must determine how important following God, through the acceptance of his son and participation in the actions and strivings of his body (the church), is to you. If it is of paramount importance, the decision is relatively easy. If not, analyze your level of commitment. In prioritizing the pursuit of God's will and purposes, the individual positions themselves to receive a multitude of blessings from the father. If the individual prays through actions seeking the face of the father, blessing and mercy follow from the throne of Grace in the lord's good timing.

Developing this prayer life takes time, patience and

perseverance to withstand the multiplicity of distractions and varied disturbances the enemy can place in our way. From crying children to blaring TVs many things fight for our attention in the modern world. One of the primary keys to building trust in the lord and his people is diligent prayer and scriptural study. For through the study of the word one learns to recognize the heart of God and his work.

Knowledge of the word is profoundly critical to defending oneself against the wiles of the enemy. Some of this knowledge can be seen through understanding the relationship between TRUST, TRUTH, and FAITH.

Trust among people comes from consistent trustworthy interaction with others over time. There can, of course, be grace-based trust on minor issues as a relationship develops. Significant-level trust among humans however often takes significant amounts of time with multiple mistakes and mishaps on the way. Faith development in God is a bit more expedient when one considers that God is infallible and does not make thoughtless or uncaring decisions or act rashly. God acts and makes decisions for the betterment of those who love him per scripture. As a result being mindful of God's tendencies and plan are often critical to developing said trust. This is why prayer, church attendance, and scripture study are so important. It never ceases to amaze me the number of people I talk to or hear about who speak fervently about wanting to hear from God yet they do not pray, read scripture, or attend church consistently. Prayer, pastoral messages, and scripture are the way God most often communicates with his people.

If we look at truth, it is far more than empirically verifiable information delivered from one person to others. Truth requires the predetermined position of honesty. A commitment to deliver all information on a topic as accurately and clearly as possible given the particular circumstance. Honesty, in many cases, requires us to open up about our own feelings. This openness requires one to be accepting of a certain level of intimacy in the interaction. For only through this kind of emotional openness can the heart truly be expressed, relational bonds be strengthened and growth occur. That is assuming, of course, that growth of the relationship is the ultimate goal. For many that is assuredly the case. Some however tend to play at faith and do not take the spiritual journey as seriously as others.

A problem with the idea of honesty is that if the information is delicate or potentially combustible, the delivery of said information is dependent on the belief that the receiver will show either grace or mercy upon reception. This can be a significant barrier to relation-ship building and intimacy development.

In "Ruthless Trust" the great Brennan Manning masterfully illuminates the distinction between Trust and faith. Faith rests in confidence in existence and purpose. Trust from this perspective involves confidence in the Will of God. Confidence in more than just the long-term plan of God but the short term, day-to-day decision making that makes up actually walking in faith is the central issue here. "The heart, converted from mistrust to trust in the irreversible forgiveness of Jesus Christ, is redeemed from the corrosive power of fear."

Fear and lack of trust in our benevolent heavenly father are the critical elements which often bind the believer from experiencing all the God has intended for his children. Key elements of the necessity of trust involve: 1) We are called to love the lord with all of our mind, soul, and strength (Luke 10:27). 2) We are also called to have faith in the Lord's existence, sovereignty, and benign intent for the well-being of the believer.

Trust in divine intent is quite different from faith in existence. This situation takes a great deal more diligence. Belief in God is one thing. Trust in God in the face of losing a five-year-old child in an accident is a different matter entirely. The faith in the existence of God is an oft reinforced concept and major portion of indoctrination and/or socialization into American culture, in many subcultures in the country. Trust in that God is a different matter which often requires very personal interactions via prayer and scriptural pursuit after God's heart.

Trust in the lord has to do, to a degree, with trust in his body on earth (i.e., the church). This is where the trouble really begins. God's followers are, unfortunately, just as flawed as the sinners they are trying to reach for the glory and growth of his kingdom. The primary difference being the TRUST and faith that the follower has developed over time in **relationship** with his heavenly father. Faith in the intent of the body of Christ is often a very tricky proposition because of the imperfection of the individual Christian and the presence of sin in the world. The church greeter who mistakenly calls a visitor to the church by a wrong name or the church counselor who has to call out a behavior as sinful are two situations which can negatively affect the seeker or new Christian. The reason people get offended or feel unduly judged by church members often has to do less with the church member and far more with the personal level of commitment and dedication to pursuit of the Heart of God within the "offended" party. Christianity is NOT supposed to be simple. It is a pursuit after holiness or "otherness," if you will. A Chase for Christ's perfection.

Trust in God's Methods

Some might say that it is easy to believe that God is benign and loving while sitting in church. When one looks at the world around us, however, that position can be challenged in light of the evil, tyranny, abusiveness and selfishness in the world. Understanding God's intention in giving man dominion over the Earth in Genesis and man's fall must be factored in when evaluating the state of the world and God's divinity and intention for his creation. God's methods for fulfilling Romans 8:28 are mysterious to us on earth because we do not see the whole picture. For if one determines, through prayer and scriptural study, that the Bible is truthful and benign in its intention, then one must appreciate the goodness and righteousness of God as he creates or allows the myriad of positive and "negative" instances which occur in one's life. I knew a woman named Christina. She is a very godly woman. Christina experienced a great deal of loss in a short period. She lost her job, a home, and finally her son in a tragic accident. Her faith through all of that astounds me to this day. She is strong in faith and steadfast in resolve. She is a hero of the faith in my personal opinion.

Looking at that acceptance of God's will as you sit reading this is likely not a tough task. When you are in the throes of pain, disappointment, loss, mourning, anger, or rage, the situation becomes much more spiritually strenuous. Many times, believers will become impatient and try to do God's work for him. We will determine that he is too busy with other things to hear us or that he is not paying attention. These are the times that prove dangerous to the spirit of the believer. Remember, God's timing is perfect. Impatience waiting for God to move is natural for the carnal mind. Remembering that the perspective of the individual believer is not God's only concern is often helpful when waiting on the Lord to move. The individual's inability to see events or situations from the viewpoint of God and our periodic losses of objectivity render individual humans as unfit to make judgements on what is best— even for ourselves!!

Christians who acknowledge their limited perspective in comparison to God's omnipotence tend to experience less stress because they hold on to the trust in God and Faith in his intentions and methods that they ALLOW to develop over time. For we must remember; God is not pushy. He does not go where he is not invited.

A Call to Arms!

So, as we look into what to do with the analyses presented, I encourage you to consider some of the pitfalls that the American Christian Church has been subject to: backstabbing and in-fighting, the gossip and distracted nature of the average Christian, debates and schisms over utterly frivolous disagreements over doctrine, and the doctrinal sea that exists between Catholicism and Protestantism. My question is this, dear reader, can we not do better than we have done so far? Have the paper-thin distinctions that divide us as believers become more important than the magnificent savior and miraculous resurrection that unites us? Here is a thought: Since Jesus said "They will know you by the way you treat one another (John 13:35)." I submit a new mindset for the Christian church in America. Put to death backbiting, gossip and slander. We must divorce yourselves from the cultural Christianity of compromise, procrastination, distraction and runaway egos. Move forward to a *relational* Christianity based on the interdependence role modeled by the disciples. This mindset empowers you and the church to build and strengthen the bonds between us. For this was role modeled for us in the Book of Acts. For in Acts the church was united, focused and driven to excel with the promised power of the Holy Spirit fueling their efforts and guiding their steps.

Pursue after the Lord with all your heart, mind and spirit. Seek his heart through prayer, meditation and study of his word. Avoid distraction which invariably leads to temptation and sin. The Father has empowered YOU with the tools needed to fulfill his will in your life. The Father loves YOU with all his heart and strength. It is your just and right act of worship to respond in kind. If you ever have a doubt that the Lord of Lords and King of Kings has called you, consider the fact that Jesus became the least of those in Israel in order to show YOU the way to eternal glory with him sheerly out of his undying love for YOU. Grace and Peace to you brothers and sisters, amen!

ABOUT ATMOSPHERE PRESS

Atmosphere Press is an independent, full-service publisher for excellent books in all genres and for all audiences. Learn more about what we do at atmospherepress.com.

We encourage you to check out some of Atmosphere's latest releases, which are available at Amazon.com and via order from your local bookstore:

Twisted Silver Spoons, a novel by Karen M. Wicks
Queen of Crows, a novel by S.L. Wilton
The Summer Festival is Murder, a novel by Jill M. Lyon
The Past We Step Into, stories by Richard Scharine
The Museum of an Extinct Race, a novel by Jonathan Hale Rosen
Swimming with the Angels, a novel by Colin Kersey
Island of Dead Gods, a novel by Verena Mahlow
Cloakers, a novel by Alexandra Lapointe
Twins Daze, a novel by Jerry Petersen
Embargo on Hope, a novel by Justin Doyle
Abaddon Illusion, a novel by Lindsey Bakken
Blackland: A Utopian Novel, by Richard A. Jones
The Jesus Nut, a novel by John Prather
The Embers of Tradition, a novel by Chukwudum Okeke
Saints and Martyrs: A Novel, by Aaron Roe
When I Am Ashes, a novel by Amber Rose

ABOUT THE AUTHOR

John is a Knoxville TN native. He earned his Bachelor's degree in Psychology from the University of Memphis and a Master's degree in Sociology from the University of Tennessee. John brings a unique perspective to the subject of the Christian walk for the American Christian. John's experience with multiple churches allows for varying viewpoints when analyzing different topics surrounding faith and behavior. He presently serves as the Director of Discipleship at Lighthouse Christian Church in Powell, TN. John is a huge TN football fan, avid bowler, and reader. John is married to his best friend, Wendy.